THOUGHTS OF THE TRANSPLANTED MISSISSIPPIAN
By
Charles M. Day III

Copyright © 2006
Charles M. Day III
All Rights reserved Through
Lulu Enterprises Inc

ISBN # 978-0-6151-6373-4

Index

YOU REST IN PEACE	…pg 11	TIME	---pg
D. U. M. B.	…pg 12	MY EYES HAVE SEEN	---pg
IT IS DONE	…pg 13	WHERE THE HEART IS	---pg
LITTLE FINGERS		LIFE	---pg
LITTLE HANDS	…pg 14	THANKS	---pg
MY LITTLE BALLERINA	…pg 15	STOP, LOOK AND LISTEN	---pg
DREAM OF GRANDEUR	…pg 16	I ENDEVOR TO SEEK HIS	
TRUTH	…pg 21	WILL	---pg
I'M AN AMERICAN	…pg 22	HAND WRITING ON	
A STILL VOICE	…pg 24	THE WALL	---pg
GOD IN OUR POCKET	…pg 20	HEAR MY WORDS	---pg 7
IRON AND STEEL	…pg 26	SPEECH	---pg 8
IT IS GONE	…pg 28	IN THE BEGINNING	
WHERE	…pg 30	AND NOW	---pg 8
I HERE AND PRAY	…pg 31	CHILDREN	---pg 8
TANGLE WITH HIM	…pg 33	BUMBLE GUMBLE	---pg 8
SHE IS SWEET	…pg 35	LOVE	---pg 8
I DO	…pg 36	A SURGEONS PRAYER	---pg 8
HALF A CENTURY	…pg 39	WORD	---pg 8
THE LIGHT	…pg 39	FATHERS	---pg 8
HIS BACK	…pg 40	REFLECTIONS	---pg 8
WHAT DO I HERE	…pg 42	THE PLACE A STEP BEHIND	---pg 8
IN HONOR OF OUR MEN AND WOMEN IN OUR ARMED SERVICES	…pg 44	FATH	---pg 8
DAWN	…pg 47	UNITED STATES BOARDER PARTROL	---pg 9
PROOF	…pg 48	THE CHOICE	---pg 9
THE CIRCLE	…pg 49	A FINAL WORD	---pg 9
AMERICA	…pg 50		
I NEEL AND I PRAY	…pg 51		
SHE SHOUTS	…pg 52		
WIFE NOBLE	…pg 53		
THE TRUTH IS	…pg 54		
HE THAT DOES			
HE THAT DOES NOT	…pg 56		
WHO IS IN CHARGE	…pg 57		
MY SON	…pg 58		
I HEAR	…pg 59		
GET IT DONE	…pg 61		

7

Prequel

  Why, was this little book written? What, will you get out of it? The answer to these two questions is partly in another question. Everybody must ask themselves from time to time this question. The question starts with "what was I doing when". What was I doing when 9-11 happened? What was I doing when President Bush was elected? This book is my answers this question for me. Yet it can answer it for you. It is about life's little occurrences during a seven year period of time and what my take on them was. You may not agree with my take on some of the subjects. However when you read this little book a thought will begin in your mind and you will have an answer to the "What was I doing when" Question. Most books take away the thinking process and put an idea of theirs in the mind of the reader. It is my effort to have people stop and think. I have made an effort toward that end. Very few books do that today.

Charles M. Day III
The Transplanted Mississippian

A good friend of mine was stricken with an undetermined ailment and was put in a wheel chair for a long while. He is the pastor of music in my church. I wrote the following letter and prose the cheer him up. God is working in both our lives and we need to follow our Lords lead wherever it goes.

Larry;
I have been through ups and downs in my life. I have been in the hospital not knowing whether I would ever get out. I was in so much pain that all I would do was wake up and push the button for my pain meds, get them and go back to sleep. No food, I did not care who was there just pain meds and sleep. In a different way I've been where you were and are now. I know you know this but I will say it anyway. This is done so you will know that God is in charge. It is not that we can do without you. It is that you have trained us so well that we can carry on as if you were there. Don't worry about us you just get well.

"YOU REST IN PEACE"

The choir still sings, a little off key.
Don't worry, you rest in peace.
Marc is planning for his phrase team to take over.
Don't worry, you rest in peace.
A committee has met to set the tonal quality of the pageant.
Don't worry, you rest in peace.
Wally has begun to direct with extraordinary flare.
Don't worry, you rest in peace.
The bases have dropped a note and the tenors have raised one.
Don't worry, you rest in peace.
Dennis is undoing redoing chicken scratches found on the music,
Don't worry, you rest in peace.
Pastor Mark is taking an active role in the music he would like to see.
Don't worry, you rest in peace.
All is going well and the choir wishes you – and well.
Don't worry, you rest in peace.
Don't let the rigors of extreme worry and panic put "rest in peace" on your tombstone.
DON'T WORRY, YOU REST IN PEACE.

Hopeful pun from
Charles M. Day III
The Transplanted Mississippian

~(*)~

Mr. President:

I hope that you have seen the report from the FCC. The FCC has given the thumbs up to the use of the "F" word on prime time radio and TV. This is the time that children will hear this word. All programs have been given the green light to us it, **ALL PROGRAMS**, unless it refers to sex. Come on now, the "F" word always refers to sex, and in a very lewd Manner. How **DUMB** can the FCC get! I have already E-mailed the FCC in protest of this decision. Michael Powell has gone too far now. I want him removed. He has shown that he does not care about decency. I would not be surprised if he has more than one porn sight on his office computer If not at his home. I don't think Michael Powell has any morals.

In my e-mail to the FCC I mused in wonder, Whether Michael Powell was concerned, if FCC stood for "**F**undamentally **C**orrupt and **C**urd". I think that someone is letting the lion in the back door. I also vented a little at him with the following prose.

D. U. M. B.

I wonder if the people at the FCC are **"Dutiful Understudies in Mental Breakdowns"**
Or if the members of the FCC are "**Drooling Unruly Mindless Babies**"!
Or is it that some of the FCC members are, "**Daffy Uncaring Mumbling Bureaucrats**".
There are honorable people in the FCC but do the ones in charge have to be, **"Dopey Underhanded Misfit Blowhards"**?
In my humble honest opinion the leaders of the FCC are just plain clueless and **DUMB.**

From the pin of
Charles M. Day III
The Transplanted Mississippian

~(*)~

FCC garbage

On November 14, 2001 I lost a very important part of my life. This was a part of my life that can never be replaced or seen again. Except for the birth of my children nothing has impacted my life more. To this day I can still hear his advice on many subjects and see his face as he would state them. The memories I have of him will have to teach me as I go through life. Though I have my faith in Christ the knowledge of this loss will be with me always. For him I wrote these words. I wish he could have heard them from my lips. If God will allowed it He may have.

IT IS DONE

His race is run. It is done!
Long and hard he toiled. It is done!
He was born in 28. It is done!
He lived through lean times. It is done!
He saw the darkness. It is done!
He saw the light. It is done!
He loved and lost and loved again. It is done!
He raised four children. It is done!
He walked through life his head held high. It is done!
He bowed before Christ. It is done!
I saw him to his last place of rest. It is done!
I lowered him down to that rest. It is done!
He started a new life today. It is done!
I buried - Father today.
IT IS DONE!

My father, Charles M. Day Jr., at 30 years of age, even though age and injury broke him physically his faith in God was strong to the end. At 73 His eyes were still clear and strong, and then he was gone.

       I love you DAD
       Charles M. Day III
The Transplanted Mississippian
          ~(*)~

Curiosity, they say, killed the cat. But to a child it is a path to learn. If guided properly the learning is remembered. It was so funny at times that my son was just a joy to have around. It is 02-05-01 and my son is almost a month past his 3rd birthday. What A wonder.

LITTLE FINGERS, LITTLE HANDS

Little fingers, little hands, what a joy, what a trial!
Little fingers, little hands into this, into that!
Little fingers, little hands grasping this, grasping that!
Little fingers, little hands sometimes burnt, sometime not!
Little fingers, little hands mostly safe, sometimes spanked!
Little fingers little hands Building charter, building patience.
Little fingers, little hands a parent's nightmare, a parent's pride!
Little fingers, little hands God's grace, God's plan!

An angle such as this should not have horns through his halo.

When my little Anna was taking dance I was mesmerized by her effort and love for ballet. I wrote this for her and when I see her in my mind one of the visions I see is her dancing.

MY LITTLE BALLERINA

She dances in my heart as she twirls on stage.
She dances in my heart. She is my second chance to raise.
She dances in my heart. She is love and sweetness.
She dances in my heart. She is a future placed in my guiding hands.
She dances in my heart. She is my little girl, my little ballerina.
She dances in my heart. She is a gift from the lord my God.
She dances in my heart. She is a promise fulfilled by God.
She dances in my heart. Oh that I may achieve what God wants me for her.
She dances in my heart. God, give me Wisdom to teach her.
She dances in my heart. God grant me strength to protect and guide her.
She dances in my heart. O God please raise up a hedge around her.
She dances in my heart. My little ballerina, My little girl,
SHE DANCES IN MY HEART.

~(*)~

01-14-04

Mr. President:

Every person I know has dreams that are too high to achieve. These are dreams of Grandeur. I have one very lofty one. Please follow the lines of my thought. Be entertained and I hope informed. Of all the e-mails I have sent you, I hope this one is put in your hands and read by you. I hope you post it for all to see for the good of all to have.

I'm an actor at heart. **So ACT 1 Scene 1** of.

A DREAM OF GRANDEUR

I enter from stage right in my church sanctuary. I am dressed in black overlapping leather plate medieval armor. Emblazoned on the chest peace is a white Pegasus. I wear over this a Black hooded cape with a red lining. The hood is pulled over my head. I have heavy boots on my feet and a blond cedar walking staff in my left hand. On stage is the entry to an Imaginary commander's tent. Behind the entry are two tables. One large table that is at the front of the platform; a small one is at the back of the platform. There are rolled up papers on the large table and a basin and water pitcher on the small table. I climb the three steps of the platform and enter the staging area. As I do so a boy 10 or 11 years of age enters and calls to me.
"Commander, commander the enemy is beginning to move. I've come to warn you of their movement."

I answer, "Don't worry lad it's not their time to move yet. This is a false action to put us off guard. This is what I want you to do. Go to the high place and sit. Take some food and water and watch them from there. When you see their torches begin to gather in the center of their encampment and next begin to slowly go to the front lines. Then you come and tell me. "

He turns to leave and I speak again.

"Oh! Lad, have you heard if the replacements have arrived. "

He speaks.

"Sir, I have heard they have arrived but I have not seen them."

"Good, now go son and keep your eyes open."

"Yes sir, right away sir."

The lad leaves and I enter the staging area and go to the small table. There I lay my staff against the table and pour water into the basin. I remove the hood and reveal I am wearing a steel helm. This I remove and set on the table. I dipped my hands into the water and wash my face and hands. I dry them with a towel and walk to the larger table. I unroll a map and begin to study it. I look up and see the audience. I pause moment and say

."At last you have arrived. Each of you is needed and each of you will have a different and very important assignment.

Some of these assignments will be tough and some not nice. Each however must be done. The army of Satan is on the move; we must stop them at the river and hold them there. The battle is the Lords and he will be victorious.

The chairman of the National Education Association has sworn the he will inflict our children by establishing a course on, "How to be a homosexual". This course will be placed in all public schools starting in kindergarten. This must not happen. We must protest this action at all levels of government.

The homosexual lobby is moving to declare Gay Unions as true marriages so they can have the same rights as other married couples. We must support the Marriage Amendment, which states that marriage is the union of one man and one woman."

As I am speaking a man gets up and walks away. I ask
"Are you leaving and why?"
He turns and speaks." I am leaving because I do not want to hear your words of hate."

"Words of hate" says I"

"Yes" he says, "I am the chairman of the local Education board. You do not want to allow the homosexual to be what he is. That is hate. You are against homosexual marriage as a way to beat down the homosexual. It is just pure hate."

As I faced this man I speak with power.

"In this country anyone can be what he or she wishes to be. I do not dispute that. However, no one can teach our children subjects that we as parents do not approve of. As for marriage, that is a union given by God Almighty to his people for the life style which God himself setup for his

people. Marriage is a triune life style, one man, and one woman in a lifetime communion with GOD. It is a holy institution not to be tampered with by man.

"But that is teaching hate to your children and denying the homosexual a full measure of life. "He says.

"No" say I," To teach the truth is not hate."

He speaks, "Your truth. There is more than one point of view. Teaching your truth is teaching hate.

"There is but one truth and it is the truth for all." Say I, "God has given, we Christians two (2) mandates. The first is that we as Christians cannot conscience or support in any way shape or form the life style of homosexuality. The second mandate says we must show the Homosexual the <u>love of Christ and give him the right to choose</u>. If he Chooses Christ and gives up the old way. We must accept him into our lives. If he chooses the old way, we must kick his dust from our feet and walk away. But the offer of the Lord Christ will always be there until God Himself takes it away. It is God's way or Mans way that is the only choice.

"You're wrong! There are more choices than that. I am leaving; I want no part of this.'
As he leaves I speak.

"Man has many ways and many paths to follow. Christ said "I am the way the truth and the light, no one comes unto the Father except by me."

I turn to the audience and look with concern. I speak.

"Another problem is about to be pushed hard by Satan's Harpies. Abortion is the murder of the unborn. A national effort is being mounted to prevent parents for being notified if their child is pregnant and an abortion is to be performed"

As I am speaking a lady gets up and begins to leave. I stop and then I speak to her.

"Is something wrong? May I help you?
She turns to me.

"Yes, something is and I am leaving."

"Why" I asked

"I am the chair woman of the National center of Planned Parenthood. You want to interfere with the woman's right to choose."

"You mean the right of a woman to kill her baby."

"No, it is not a baby until it is fully born. Until then it is a bunch of cells or a fetus but not a baby."

"Madam", say I." We have a saying here in the south. If it walks like a duck and it has feathers like a duck. If it quacks like a duck and it looks like a duck. It's got to be a DUCK.

If it is made of a human ovum and a human sperm whether it is in Petri dish or a woman's womb it is a human baby. It makes no difference if it is two cells or 20 cells or a fully formed body. It is still a baby; to take its life is murder.

The American Medical Association has stated that <u>with proper</u> prenatal care abortion is not necessary. The AMA also states that there is no medical necessity or reason to perform Partial Birth Abortion. It is proven however that a greedy doctor can make thousands of dollars in six months by selling baby parts to research companies.

Most of these companies are out of this country where the laws that prohibit the practice can't touch them. The only proven reasons for abortion are convenience and money."

She walks out saying "Your wrong."

I watch her as she leaves then my eyes cross to the audience. As I look at the audience I notice nine (9) robed people in the front row just listening to me. I look at them and I speak.

"As to the nine (9) persons seated before me. I have read the letter written by Thomas Jefferson and I purpose to change one word in that letter. That word is church. I will change it to a word that has more practical meaning today. That word is denomination. Jefferson was not talking about a wall of separation between God and state because he knew that you could not separate the Lord God and our government. He was referring to the differences between the denominations or sects in our country. He did not want to offend one denomination in preference over another.

Jefferson believed in God and sought after God for advice in his life, as did Washington and Adams.

If you will look at the charter of the vary building in which you hold your court sessions. That charter states that the building is to be used for court sessions on weekdays and church services on Sunday. Your court building is a very large church. But you know this don't you, and it is the last thing that you want this country to know. Right!

The last sentence of Jefferson's original draft of the Letter is a clause, which he left out in the final draft because he did not want to offend anyone group. It states!"Discipline of each respective sect!"

How respectful this president was. In no way did Jefferson wish to separate church and our Government. He went on and thanked the people for Their prayers and would pray for them as well. Does this sound like a separation of church and state? Thomas Jefferson is actually asking for prayer that he might do a good job in office.

The facts are that you are basing your judgments on a misunderstanding and the lies of anti-God zealots. You cannot successfully separate God and this Government, because this Government is, as our Fore Father wanted it to be. That is our laws and our Government, are based on God's precepts and rules. Stating it any other way is a falsehood!

I turn and go to the little table and retrieve my helm and staff. The boy enters and alerts me to the enemy movement. As I leave the little window in my staff lights up and I look at the audience and say.

'The light of the Lord my God is here. The battle is his."

I then leave the room.

I said this was a dream. I pray to God that it will come true for someone even if it does not come true for me.

GREAT THINGS

I dream of great things, I do the little things.
I dream of great deeds of valor, I do needed things of necessity.
I dream of fighting for God and Country, I teach lessons to my little ones As God would have it done.
I have done one great thing. I bowed down to the Cross and gave, myself to the one who gave his all for me.

A Thought form
Charles M. Day III
The transplanted Mississippian

I was reading a news article when a statement by a person writing the article struck me as odd. It was "Truth is not the same thing from one person to the next. It is basically relative and does not exist," I composed this prose for that person. Yet I could never get it to him. Maybe he will read it here. If it will do any good I hope others will read and understand what is said.

TRUTH

Truth is not hidden, unless it is done on purpose.
Truth is an aid; it relaxes the worry and uncertainty of life and allows action or closure.
Truth is solid and immovable, it waits silently to be discovered and used.
Truth is like an arrow that pierces the heart of its target.
Truth is never a lie or ill advised.
Truth is truth.
Truth is to be used by anyone to right wrongs, heal wounds and beat back darkness.
Truth is a sharp two-edge sword in the hands of a champion warrior.
Truth is despised by the wicked.
Truth has stumbled in the streets of our country because of the wicked.
"When Truth is nowhere to be found, who ever shuns evil becomes a pray. " ISA 59:15
O my God, "I hold fast to you statutes, O lord; do not let me or <u>my country</u> be put to shame."Ps.119; 30-31

A phrase form
Charles M. Day III
The Transplanted Mississippian

~(*)~

01-07-04

Mr. President:

You have come up with a bad idea this time. Let me tell you a true story to illustrate what I mean. In late 2002 and early 2003, in Jackson Mississippi and the surrounding cities were hit with a series of severe storms, several tornados and hailstorms. As bad as this was there was a silver lining to it. These storms presented a chance to the local small businessmen.

It was a good chance to earn a good living. The insurance companies were paying to rebuild and re-roof homes. There was enough work to keep every local builder, roofer, tree service company and landscaper busy for at least a year or more. This was very good. You see I do tree service and when things are slow. I do landscaping and roofing as well. I am a very small operation which is made up of me and one or two helpers. So I need to do more than one thing.

The beginning of 2003 was very good with all the available work. But by June things started to slow down fast. I started to catch up on my bills and it looked as if I would get a little ahead. Then the slowdown and the jobs started to vanish. I was barely able to pay bills, no savings, no setting aside for Christmas, on extras, NOTHING. My wife had bought a few things for our children for Christmas at the beginning of the year but not much. By October all work had stopped no work at all. The larger companies had several months' of work but nothing like at the beginning of the year. I did very little work after April of 2003, a smattering of little jobs and one roof in November. It was enough to pay one month's rent and utilities. I was now two month behind in rent.

Here we are in January of 2004. I've been dead in the water sense the last job in November. I'm now three months behind in rent. Monthly bills are coming in and no money to pay them. To top it all off my loving wife of 10 years and mother of my two children, 4 and 10 years of age, had to enter the hospital for extensive abdominal surgery. I had to ask for state aid for this. At this time I still don't know if the state will help. I don't have any insurance. I can't afford it. I am 53 years of age and because I am of this age no one wants to hire me. My little company is all we have. I could ask my church for help but they have done so much for me to date. I feel that they will think I am not trying hard enough. If it were not for my church and two members of my family my children would not have had a good Christmas. Through these people the lord my God was good to us.

Why did my business fall so fast? The reason was twofold.

1. Several Hispanic crews moved in from Texas. Each crew was made up of 10 to 20 members and a foreman. The foreman paid each crew man $65 per day plus room. No board.

2. The average pay in Mississippi for a roofer is $15 an hour or $30 a square. On average a good roofer can nail down correctly 15 to 20 squares a day. Cheap labor and lots of it killed the work in this area in six months. Now the larger companies have a lot of work they can afford to hire these Hispanic crews and think nothing of it. The little guys like me are going under fast. There is nothing we can do.

The kicker is these Hispanic crews are taken back to Texas and replaced with new workers every three to four months to keep them from getting better jobs. Most of them do not speak any or very little English. I will state that most if not all of these Hispanic crewmen are Illegal.

Now I hear that you are going to allow illegal aliens to stay in this country and literally give them a free ride. This SIR is a load or recycled Anal Patties. I finally found a small job working for someone else which would give me a small paycheck. Too little, maybe too late! I have most likely lost my little company. I am willing to do these little jobs, which make a hard living. The actions that you have taken are removing the work from me.
Thank You Sir, for nothing.

Sir I know you are a good man and I know you are trying to do a good job. But I feel that someone is leading you down the wrong path. Please wake up before it is too late. I want you there where you are, but it hurts when thing like this happen.

I 'M AN AMERICAN

I 'm an American hard at work, don't take my work away!
I 'm an American standing tall, don't cut me down!
I am an American willing to work. Don't turn me away!
I'm an American strong at heart. Don't cut it out!
I'm an American running to the call. Don't trip me!
I am an American ready to do my duty. Don't block my way!
I'm an American true Red, White, and Blue. Don't fade my colors!
I am an American, So are you!
 WHY! DO YOU DO WHAT YOU DO?

A cry from
Charles M. Day III
The Transplanted Mississippian

~(*)~

Mr. President;

Today was more or less like yesterday. Tonight I went to church for the choir retreat. Every year it is around the 18th of December. Colonial Heights Baptist Church does a Christmas production that lasts for 5 days ending on Sunday afternoon.

Well, there was a dinner before hand, the cost was $4 for each adult and children eat free. I should have known that eating too much would affect me that way, yet I indulge. I was so full I had no control over my voice. I could not hit the right notes and if I did hit them the volume was ether to weak or too strong. I was so bad that the choir director tried to correct it. It is Embarrassing to say the least.

Ok what did I learn? I let one of the Seven Deadly Sins (Gluttony) prevent me from praising God. God did not get praise by me and now I feel as if I missed out on an opportunity of service. Oops!!! I am about to let another one of the deadly sins to creep in, Sloth. When you are in the middle self-pity party you avoid physical and spiritual work. You find out when you open the door to one, the other six try to creep in.

Sir, I hope you are better at avoiding the 7deadly sins and powers of helplessness. Yet there is a good way to combat these seven. God has given us several ways to overcome them. They are the Contrary, Theological, Heavenly cardinal virtues and the 7 corporal works of mercy.

The Cardinal virtues are **Prudence, temperance, Courage, and justice**. Classical Greek philosophers considered these to be the foremost virtues. Christian theologians agreed and considered these to be equally important to all people, weather they were Christian or not.

The theological virtues are Love, hope, and Faith. These are considered to be of Divine Order. Because of man's fall from grace these three are not natural to man. They are however conferred upon man after **accepting** grace form Jesus Christ.

The seven Contrary Virtues are Humility, Kindness, Abstinence, Chastity, Patience, Liberality and Diligence. These 7 virtues were introduced by the Philosopher Prudentius, sometime around the year 410 in his poem "Pschomachia", (Battle for the soul). He said practicing these would protect you against the 7 deadly sins.

The seven Heavenly Virtues are Faith, Hope, Charity, Fortitude and Prudence, justice and temperance. These are a combination of the Cardinal and Theological Virtues.

The 7 corporal works of mercy are- Feed the hungry, Give drink to the thirsty, Give shelter to strangers, clothe the naked, Visit the sick, Minister to prisoners and bury the dead. I guess that what it comes down to is God
has a better way that is a 1000% better every time. He has a still voice that we should listen to.

A STILL VOICE

I feel unable to move. I am week.
    A still voice says, USE MY STRENGTH.
The load is too heavy and I am weary.
    A still voice says. I AM HERE LET ME HELP YOU.
The journey is too long, I am afraid.
    A sill voice says. I WILL PROTECT YOU.
The river is too wide I can't cross.
    A still voice says. Let me part the waters.
Whatever, I cannot do.
    A still voice says. I CAN.
Whatever, I cannot be.
    A still voice says. Let me help.
Whatever, I am not.
    A still voice says. I AM.
I don't know the way.
    A still voice says. FOLLOW ME.
By myself I can do little or nothing at all.
    A still voice says. WITH ME AT YOUR SIDE YOU CAN DO ALL THINGS.
I have nothing.
    A still voice says. I WILL, PROVIDE AS YOU REQUIRE.
I have no one to turn to.
    A still voice says. TRUST IN ME.
I am alone! I have no one!
    A still voice says. I AM YOU FATHER, COME INTO MY ARMS.
I weep for joy.

Praise from
Charles M Day III
The Transplanted Mississippian

~(*)~

10-26-03

    I have two children still at home, Anna age 10 and Sterling age 4. Both have songs of the heart, Anna in dance and sterling in voice. They are both growing up to fast for my liking. I want them to slow down but that won't happen. I'm afraid that they will lose their song of the heart. Proverbs 22:6 says "Train a child up in the way he should go and when they are old they will never leave it."

    That is not what we, as parents have done in this country. We are losing our right to worship God, because we have not taught our children proper Christian values. The right to pray in public or to show a Bible in your position is being taken away. To say the word God in a government building is becoming a crime all because we have not raised our children to love and fear the Lord our God. The problem that we are having today is both social and personal, steams from a lack of belief in a Moral God.

GOD IN OUR POCKET

In the hustle and bustle of our world, we have a god that fits in our pocket.
We don't worry about what we do. We have a god in our pocket.
He does not see our little white sins, this god in our pocket.
He brushes away our big sins with a wag of his finger, this god in our pocket.
It is convenient thing to have, this god in our pocket.
EL ELYON, the "Most High" God, looks down from above. He won't fit in your Pocket.
EL SHADDI. "All sufficient one" needs nothing from us. H won't fit in your pocket.
ADONOI-YAHWEN," Lord Master", leader of all. He will not fit in your pocket.
JEHOVAH-NISSI, "Thee My Miracle, Lord My Banner", will protect us. He won't fit in your pocket.
JEHOVAL RAAH, "Lord my shepherd, Leads us, he does not follow". He won't fit in your pocket.
EL OHIM, "God, Judge, Creator", hates sin period. He won't fit in your pocket.
EL OLAM, God the universe of ancient days", fills the expanses. He won't fit in your pocket.
The great I AM is far beyond your minds ability.
HE WILL NOT FIT IN ANY POCKET.

~(*)~

This was written for the President of the USA, friends and any man who has a daughter. It is one reason for a father to want to live from day to day as well as for the Glory of God.

IRON AND STEEL

To you the Daughters of man, falls a very important job.
To you falls a duty and responsibility.
In a man's life there are many things that form his core.
A man is a man because of these things.
To face the world there must be a strong base.
A foundation in God!
A path of purpose!
A wife of character and Children of the future!
From our daughters, a father needs a touch of love to strengthen his shoulders.
A kiss on his cheek, to soften his expressions and relax his wrinkled brow.
A hug to ease a worried day.
An impish smile to brighten an otherwise dull day.
A son is a mark of pride, which not all men have.
A daughter must be protected while young.
Because it is a man like daddy she will wed.
A daughter will show the world what the man is made of.
A daughter will show his character, his strength and his way.
A daughter is spring and light to a father.
A daughter is honor and truth.
A daughter gives purpose to his daily grind.
But a daughter turns a man into IRON AND STEEL.
A father for her sake he must be a man of IRON AND STEEL.
A daughter's duty is to keep him that way.

From the pen of a father
Charles M. Day III
The transplanted Mississippian

~(*)~

01-02-04

Mr. President:

A thought has occurred to me that is, very crazy. But what if Osama Ben Loden is not where we think he is. What if he is right under our noses! Step back, a moment and think out of the box for a while and take hold of this crazy idea. Is he hiding in the most obvious place? Places that we would not expect? Maybe he is hiding next to one of our installations in a country that we have a base of operation. Or is he in an embassy not too friendly to us in that country. How about an even crazier idea! Right here in the good old USA. The news says that there is a lot of chatter going on in the world. May be this is what some of it means. Our boarders are for all intense and purpose is open to any illegal that crosses it. Anyone can step across either the Mexican or Canadian border at any time with little or no opposition. Federal senators and Congressman of the states that boarder Mexico do not want anything to impede the flow of illegal immigrants for political reasons. These people do not want to hear common sense. It is not to their Political advantage.

Yet, we not only are letting into our country the very people that are pulling the country down because of the social claimant where they come from. We are also allowing an opportunity for the bad element to come in as well. Don't get me wrong, **I am for the legal entry into this country** for people that will get and pay for an education so that they might go back home and improve their own country. I am also for people coming to this country to live and become a part of our way of life. I am not for the takeover of this country by sheer numbers of people that will completely change the fabric of our society, as do a few congressmen and senators. I am not for giving the lawbreakers that cross the boarders of this country, a free ride and a kiss on the cheek.

Our boarders are a mess and Yes someone like Osama Ben Loden can Easley slip into this country through our leaky boarders and set up cells and bring us down. Just think we may be handing our enemy the very way to end our way of life. Then we will become just another world-dominated nation where the people have no say.

No freedom to act as an individual or to follow a dream. That is a sad state of affairs. A state we as a country are now entering. IT IS GONE!

IT IS GONE

It is gone, the right to worship God in Public.
It is gone, the right to work and earn a living.
It is Gone is the right to live in safety.
It is gone, the right to life within secure boards.
If we as Americans don't take our place and object and demand what is right under God's law.
Then we will say. It is gone, THE HEDGE OF SAFETY "THE LORD OUR GOD" PUT AROUND THIS COUNTRY.

A Thought from
Charles M. Day III
The Transplanted Mississippian
~(*)~

Mr. President;

    I wonder if a few things are breaking out. The Democratic Party is making much ado about something. What I don't know. I think Senator Clinton should be watched closely and politically neutralized if her momentum begins to build. You have Saddam's fighters second-guessing themselves. The new countries that have sent troops are learning the cost of freedom and what it entails. Don't stop pushing Saddam's people. I think that Syria and Iran need to be warned off. They still pose a large and serious problem.

    Sir, don't let your guard down, too many things are moving at once. I think it is time that you corner Ted Kennedy and the senate minority leader Mr. Tom Dasheal with a few key republican supporters and take them on a federal look to see Iraq for a first hand facts mission. I would include Kennedy and Dasheal because they need to see the truth, Not that they would repeat it truthfully or not try to slant it into their favor. Don't hide anything from them let them see it. I do not believe they will go. I feel that they are chickens and will find excuses not to go.

    However I am glad that you are in the Oval Office Big Chair and doing that good job. I need to feel that God has you there doing this job.

WHERE

Where am I?
Where have I come from?
Where should I be?
Where is my place in this world?
Where should I go?
Where should I do what I must do?
Where should I begin?
Where should I end?
"WHERE"? Can only be answered by God!
God is the beginning and the end.
God is fulfillment and the fulfiller.
God is the life eternal, from everlasting to everlasting.
The answer is beyond a shadow of a doubt,
The Lord our God, Christ Jesus the son, The Eternal Holy   Spirit,
The three that are "One"!

        A God given insight from Charles M Day III
            The Transplanted Mississippian

~(*)~

Mr. President:

    Today was pretty much like last week. At least were work is concerned, few bids, no work and no money. I read that Israel attacked the Gaza strip and killed 11 people. It is sad that innocent people have to die. However, there is this hate the Islamic countries have for any other religion, including ours (Christianity).

    I know, you know this, but I have to say it out loud. The Islamic religion will not be satisfied until the world is Islamic. They mean the destruction of every religion except theirs. They are teaching in the Muslim academies and schools that are here in the USA, That America is an evil country and that we American's are worse than nothing. They are teaching that Christ will come back and break the cross and convert everybody to Islam. How is that for backstabbing action! We are allowing a school in the United States to teach treason.

    Then there is Louis Farrakhan Teaching hate in this country from his pulpit. His efforts on the pulpit are boarder line Treason if anything. Ok, now take the statements of several of our so-called movie stars (idols) who are saying out loud that this country deserved 9-11 and hopes that the US gets kicked again. Mr. President this is getting scarier by the minuet. It seems that the Christians are being lambasted from every side. If it is not the humanist or atheist saying there is no God, or the scientific community spouting evolution and that proves there is no God. It's the 9th circuit court stating that the mention of God in the pledge of allegiance in any public school is unconstitutional. Which, by the way, is a damn lie? If I did not have my faith in God I would be taking my family to the swamp and hiding out there till the second coming. Sometimes I wish I had a magic eraser and could use it to erase the problem. Good thought but I know that is not possible.

    Sir you have the power to tell that self-righteous judge in the 9th circuit court that he is wrong and if he would ever look at the history of this country he would know it. The congress of this mighty country could also tell him as well as pass a law protecting the national motto and the pledge of allegiance. However in the congress where such a bill is being considered even now, there are a few of our senators and representatives trying to stonewall that bill. I guess it is true, about power. It corrupts.

    Anyway there are two songs on an album by Marty Goetz named "HE IS MY DEFENCE" The title song has these words, "My soul wait thou only, only up on God. For from is my expectation. He is my Defense I shall not be moved. My messiah only, He is my rock and the horn of my salvation. The second is "FOR ZION'S SAKE". The words here are O Jerusalem, Jerusalem, Messiah wept for you, should we not weep too. For Zion's sake I will not keep silent. For Zion's sake I will not hold my peace. Day or night all of you who call upon the Lord, call upon the lord for Zion's sake give not rest till he makes Jerusalem praise in the earth."

     I love listening to this C D; it gives me a clear mind to Praise God and pray for others.

I HEAR AND I PRAY

I hear and I pray for the love of others.
I hear and I pray for the peace of others.
I hear and I pray for the health of others.
I hear and I pray that all men will seek the Lord my God.
I hear and I pray for those in need.
I hear and I pray that God will hear and answer my prayers.

The silhouette view of a Harrier Jet rising off the deck of the USS Coronado! Photo taken in the summer of 1970 by Airman Charles M. Day III

I can't express how wonderful Our GOD is. Can you find a word that is the right description?

A prayer from
Charles M. Day III
The Transplanted Mississippian
~(*)~

11-10-03

Mr. President:

God is handing you a large gift. The economy is turning out to be OK and the jobless rate is lower. Now you need to do something big in Iraq. I think a caution should be used here, while preparing to jump into a big effort in with a big push into the hot zones. I think the death toll can be stopped if the boarder or entries into Iraq can be watched and controlled.

Any and all people of Syrian and Iranian passports should be deported unless there is a proper reason for them being there. Syrian and Iranian passports are a dead give away to problems. Auto and tank convoys should not go from point A to Point B at brake neck speeds. Each convoy should be covered by two hellos. No hellos should go up alone there should be two or more. There should be no low flights. Go from deck to high altitude each crew keeping eyes open for trouble till they reach destination. I know, I am here not over there.

TANGLE WITH HIM

The lines were drawn. Both sides eyed one another.
The commanders were ready weapons were drawn.
One-stepped forward and shouts curses and blasphemies.
He was a real big one a monster. No one wanted to tangle with him.
He stepped forward they stepped back. No one wanted to tangle with him.
His weapon was three times the size of any of theirs. No one wanted to tangle with him.
As his steps quacked the earth as he walked. No one wanted to tangle with him.
Here I am show me your best, his voice thundered. No one wanted to tangle with him.
With his mind on EL ELYON, one had no fear. "I'll tangle with him."
My faith is in YAHWEH, He is not so big, and "why should I worry. I'll tangle with him."
A bag of hot air, there is no worry there. "I have JEHOVAH-NISSI. I'll tangle with him."
I have JEHOVAH SABAOTH, with one shinny stone and the giant is dead.
"I tangled with him."
The giant's head in his hand held high as David shouts
"KANNA is my armor and, NO ONE CAN TANGLE WITH HIM!"
"In my heart I have ELOHM. With any giant I can tangle."
DO YOU? CAN YOU?

From the pen of
Charles M Day III
The Transplanted Mississippian

~(*)~

A Painting of David holding Goliath's head after defeating him.

To compare true love to false love is the theme of this next poem.

SHE IS SWEET

She is sweet, your love, your companion, and your wife.
She is sweet, and is an increase in your life, your wife.
She is sweet, as well, the temptress.
She is sweet, as well but she drains you strength and shorted your life, the temptress.
She is sweet; She gives to you joy, your wife.
She is sweet; the future is blessed in her hands, your wife.
She is sweet; her joy is hollow, the temptress.
She is sweet; her future leads to death, the temptress.
She is sweet; her hands are busy for your sake, your wife.
She is sweet; the fruit of her womb is a joy to you, your wife.
She is sweet; her hands are in the belly of deceit, the temptress.
She is sweet; the fruit of her womb is a bitter burden, the temptress.
She is sweet; which sweet is your sweet.
"As a loving deer and a graceful doe, let her breasts satisfy you at all times, and always be enraptured in her love. For why should you, my son, be enraptured by an immoral woman, and be embraced in the arms of a seductress." Prov. 5:19&20

Joan Ann (Day) Willis

Mother of five and friend of many.

A Memory from
Charles M. Day III
The Transplanted Mississippian

~(*)~

11-22-03

Mr. President;

I want to scream, shout, rant and rave. The news media and the entire selected interviewed persons are dancing around the truth. They are afraid to state the truth. The Homosexual propionates say that marriage should be given equally to all who want it. It means equal rights under the law. This is a **lie!** The homosexuals already have equal protection under the law. They just want to have it all their way without opposition.

The de-sanctification of the institution of marriage is one of the steps in destroying the Christian way of life. This is a way of life that has been the stability of this nation for over 200 years. The homosexual way of life is a dead end life style.

As Christians we are mandated by God to shun, stay away from and not acknowledge the homosexual way of life. However we are also mandated by God to embrace the homosexual and show him the way to salvation. Not by force but by gentle love, allowing the homosexual to decide if he wants Christ's grace or not. This is a frightening concept to the progenitors of the homosexual life style, because it means the END of their life style.

God has stated through his word, The Bible, and his deeds with us that the permanent, till natural death do they part, marriage between one man and one woman IN COMMUNION WITH GOD, "A TRIUNE RELATIONSHIP" is the blessed life style. Any other life style is wrong.

The only way that the homosexual life style can increase their numbers is by recruiting young people. This means to teach our children their ways and to erode our way of life by replacing the truth with a lie.

Marriage is a true Christian institution. It has been handed down through time to us as a gift from GOD. It is to be used with respect to God the giver. It is because of this point that Marriage is being used by, the homosexual community and their supporters, as a way to seek legitimacy and drive a wedge into Christianity in an effort to bring it down.

At the most recent NEA conventions the president of the NEA made an effort to install rules and regulations that would setup courses that would teach all children in public schools starting in kinder garden all the way up through high school on "how to be a homosexual". Because of the protest across this country and a protest rally outside the convention center hosting the NEA, he did not succeed. Leaving the convention the NEA president swore to have the course in place and taught in all public schools across this country. He stated that, "I don't care about the wishes of the parents of school children. It is my duty to see to it that this course be taught."

This is a, sometimes silent and sometimes vocal war. But it is a war. One that all true believing Christians must actively fight. Efforts are being made to prevent ministers from teaching the word of God's point of view on homosexuality from the pulpit. The silencing of God's people is opening the door to where the homosexual community can have indiscriminate sex with anyone they can. Age makes no difference to them. Homosexuals will have sex with 6 or 7 year old boys and girls. What do they care!

The homosexual community **demands an open door policy for their every whim and desire**, regardless of what you hear them say. The average Homosexual does not care about truth or decency he or she only cares about their perverse desire. The majority of the homosexual population prefers, the young child because they are more pliable to their sexual desires. They do not care anything about the child's welfare. If you can find one homosexual that does not act upon these desires one or more times in their lifetime, there are at least 10,000 that will and do.

To answer Mr. Bill O'Reilly of "The Factor" fame, when he asked what is wrong with a gay couple adopting a child?" and he also stated just recently. "I don't see the Problem with gay marriage, it doesn't bother or effect me but the law forbids it by a decision of 60% of the people of this country."

The answer to the first statement is this. It is wrong to place a child in a home that will lead this child into harm's way. The highest suicide rate is among the homosexual community. The highest domestic crime rate is in the homosexual community. I don't care if this gay couple is the pillar of the community. To place a child in a sinful and harmful way of life is wrong. Christ said   **"It is better for a man to put a millstone around his neck and jump into the sea than it is to place a child in sin."**

The answer to the second question is. Marriage is an institution that is SET ASIDE BY GOD ALMIGHTY for a man to join with a woman for a lifetime together in communion with God. It is called a Tri-union state of being. Man, Woman and GOD! For us to allow miss use of this gift of God is an insult and the Homosexual population knows this very well. The very act of homosexuality is a DECLARED SIN BY GOD. READ YOU'RE CANNON!! PERIOD END OF SUGJECT!!!!

I DO

GOD says, to commit is to say I DO.
GOD says, to take to one's self another life is to say I DO.
GOD says, to open your heart to another is to say I DO.
GOD said to us "Follow me and I will say I DO."
GOD said, "Take my hand and I will say I DO.
No matter what we have done God always says "I DO."
GOD'S direction is that one man is to cleave to one woman in marriage and say I DO.
GOD set marriage aside for one man to marry one woman for life and say. I DO.
I repeat, GOD says, to commit, to take, to open your heart, to marry, to follow GOD, and to say I DO.
To set aside the will of GOD is to say NO to GOD.
But if you come back to him GOD says I DO.

A thought from
Charles M. Day III
The Transplanted Mississippian

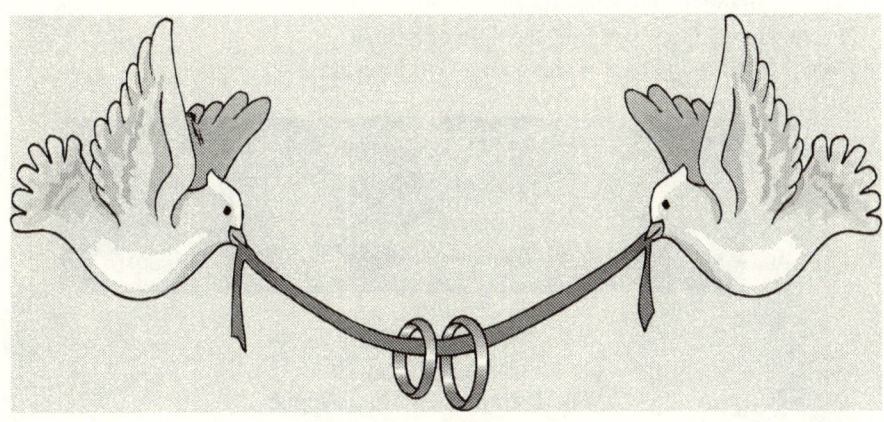

I wrote this prose in honor of a friend Sergeant Jeff Rudd's fiftieth birthday. He enjoyed it.

HALF A CENTURY

Time is a problem and an asset. But in half a century! Well?
Most wine ages with good taste, But in half a century! I don't know.
Bananas get sweeter as they age. But in half a century! I don't think so.
Honey becomes stronger as it ages. But in half a century! AHHHH
Wisdom grows with age. But in half a century! It has some volume.
Knowledge compounds with age. But in half a century! The interest may be too much
Gray hair comes with age. But in half a century! I think I will leave that one alone.
Wrinkles appear with age. But in half a century! No cream will work.
Bodies ache with age. But in half a century! There isn't enough Ben Gay.
Life mellows with age. But in half a century it may be too flat.
Yet after a half a century is age good or bad? It may take another 50 years and an act of God to find out.
Are you up to ANOTHER HALF CENTURY?

~(*)~

Written for a contest on portry.com poetry bash I did not win, but I had fun.

THE LIGHT

To walk in the light is an honor.
To serve in the light is redeeming.
To be in the light seeking after you is fulfilling.
To stay in the light is a blessing.
From you my God comes all the light of heaven.
May I dwell in the light with you my God forever!

A Thought of
Charles M. Day III
The Transplanted Mississippian

~(*)~

11-08-03

Mr. President:

The elections are beginning to heat up. Everybody in the Democratic Party is trying to show how honorable they are. They also take cheap shots at you and what you are trying to do. That shows just how shallow they really are. I know that Iraq is a hard subject to talk about. I think that you should listen very closely to what your detractors are saying. The skill is to answer their charges in a point-by-point manner. You want look bad, if you open up full-scale operations in Iraq, to hunt down Saddam or Ben Laden, where ever they are. The thing is doing the job you need to do and doing it right and with graceful quickness. If the Democrats say "look you made a mistake and you are trying to correct it." Let them say it. Just say to them "Even if that is true, WHAT OF IT! I am trying to do the job right. You with all of your heehawing and finger pointing could not do any better, Period."

I know that the jobless rate went down. This should show your detractors that you had the right Idea on that subject. I just pray that you turn to the scriptures more every day for inspiration and solace. There, God may guide you as I know he does.

Sir, I wish I could do more for you than send you e-mail to show my appreciation and respect for you. Yet, this is what I do for you and I hope they do help you. I hope that there is nether the frying pan or the fire for you as punishment just for doing your job for this nation.

The way I see it is that you must do the job and all thing the way God would have it. Or the LORD will turn his back on us. I don't want to see **HIS BACK.**

HIS BACK

I often look into the sky and see God smile from on high.
    I pray never to see his back.
I see his joy in the trees the flowers and the grasses.
    I pray never to see his back.
I feel the life he gave me, and the wonders that I see.
    I pray never to see his back.
I revel in the joy of the children he gave me.
    I pray never to see his back.
I loving lay next to the wife he gave me.
    I pray never to see his back.
When Israel suffered in those early days God had turned his back.
In the history of old Israel when it did not rain for seven years,
    God had turned his back.
When Israel turned form God's ways and sought their own, they failed.
    God had turned his back.
When Christ Jesus took the sins of all mankind, on himself,
That, all men, could claim salvation and a place in heaven.
The world stood still, grew cold and dim.
    God had turned his back.
I pray to walk in the light of the Lord my God. To seek his face and love,
And above all else!!! I PRAY NEVER TO SEE HIS BACK.

        A Thought of
        Charles M. Day III
        The Transplanted Mississippian

~(*)~

Creation of Adam on the ceiling of the Sistine Chapel.

11-15-03

Mr. President;

      You are about to make an effort to show the British people that you are right, justified or had cause to deal with Iraq. Don't do it. If the people you speak to don't want to hear what you have to say, they won't. If you must, I think you should just show what you have found and can prove. That alone should be proof enough. I don't think that your advisors are paying enough attention to what is going on in this country and around the world. That means that you are not getting the proper information. I think you should do as the old adage says and "stop and smell the flowers." Take some time off, a day or two and just listen to what is being said. Don't act on anything, don't react, just listen.

      Listen to all the news channels and take notes. Walk down town wherever you are and listen to the people in the coffee shops, or at the local McDonalds, just listen. Don't hand this off to someone else, do **it yourself**. If you do this you will find out where you really are. Here's an idea, pick up a phone book to any city and **YOU** call five or ten people in that city at random. Ask them what is on their mind and what haunts them. Take notes; get the feelings for **yourself**. You will know better what is needed. When you let someone else do these types of work for you all the time you lose touch with the people you represent. You must do some of this yourself then your aids can do the rest.

WHAT DO I HEAR

I walk and look but do I is see or hear?
I walk about my work. Do I hear what is said around me?
I step through a door. Will I listen to what might be, on the other side?
I walk through the woods. Do I listen to the rustle of the leaves?
I want to live not die. Do I listen to those that know?
When God speaks do I listen? Do I hear?
TO LISTEN IS TO KNOW. TO KNOW IS TO LIVE FULLY AND WISELY.

                  A thought of
                Charles M. Day III
          The Transplanted Mississippian

If you listen to what is going on around you. You can learn much. The drawing of the three crosses on Calvary (Golgotha, the skull.) by Charles M. Day III below was done in this manner to magnify, this one event in human history. It was done in a full painting that hung in his grandmother's hall for many years till her death in 1977.

A color sketch by
CHARLES M DAY III

~(*)~

I wrote a series of prose to honor the armed services. Yet one group of men and women, have not been honored to my knowledge with praise of their efforts to protect this country. So I wrote a Praise in prose to honor them and added it to the prose of the five branches of the armed forces of the United States. The Original five I gave to Lt. Col. Oliver North when he visited our church on the 4th of July 2003. Please enjoy the praises of our **Navy, Coast Guard, Marines, Army, Air Force and the United States Border Patrol.**

I sent a copy of these poems to the Pentagon. The poems were very well received and are now hanging in the Pentagon.

CHAIRMAN OF THE JOINT CHIEFS OF STAFF
WASHINGTON, D.C. 20318-9999

16 May 2006

Mr. Charles M. Day III
PO Box 355
Tribune, Kansas 67879

Dear Mr. Day,

　　Thank you for the framed poems in honor of our Armed Services. I will be sure to hang them in one of our offices for our Service men and women to see.

　　I truly appreciate your thoughtfulness and continued support of our great Nation. Best wishes in all your future endeavors.

　　　　　　　　　Sincerely,

　　　　　　　　　PETER PACE
　　　　General, United States Marine Corps
　　　　　　　　　Chairman
　　　　　　of the Joint Chiefs of Staff

In Honor of our Men and Women in our armed services I give these six poems.

NAVY

Ocean wave, foam and steel!
Brave men and women manning gun and wheel;
Flesh and blood in diligence, to search and see,
They stand ready in raging swell or becalmed sea.
To those who would threaten you and me,
They sail near and far to bring the battle by air and sea.
To plant the flag of freedom, justice and truth,
This with pain and death is given to our budding youth.
Look out to their pure and honored dress white ranks.
For us all and for their sakes pray to God and give them thanks.

COAST GUARD

Born to patrol and guard our coast from smugglers and foreign Hosts!
They ride through a boiling waters, rough swells, shot and shell.
Night and day they save lives at the risk of their own.
Fighting smugglers and crime with a vigorous and steady tone!
They watch over traffic in the shipping lanes and on the high sea.
Fighting fires, giving aid, and watching over you and me!
SEMPER PARATUS, ALWAYS READY, this is their cry.
For this country, they guard, they save, they fight and they die.
Give thanks to God for these men and women of coastal blue.
For without them, there is no freedom for me and you.

MARINES

For battle at sea they were born.
From there they took the battle to shores of sand.
There, to fight and die in many a foreign land.
To show their strength of purpose with honor in mind,
For duty and honor they did their task and left many behind.
To battle, they sail and march in hot days and cold nights.
They serve us by defending our freedom and rights.
No complaint is heard from their young lips.
As they fight and die for this country as its future it grips.
Let us fall on our knees and pray to God Almighty,
That these men and women in blue and red, are in God's safety

ARMY

Marching in forest and swamp, over hill and dale.
They fight the bitter fight and die in a bullet hail.
To defend us in battle and guard us in foreign lands,
We place our safety in their capable hands.
To look toward the future when there is no war,
They march forward into the enemy's bore.
For this country they are called and they are sent.
For truth Justice and Honor their blood is spent.
To God w give thanks and praise over what we have seen.
May God protect these brave men and women in green!

UNITED STATES BOARDER PATROL

In wooded splendor and desert heat, they keep our boarders safe.
Through longest day and endless night,
They watch to stop drug lords and terrorist alike.
No fear is shown as they do their job though death is close at hand.
Nothing will stop the steadfast duty of this fearless band.
Standing, with dignity and honor not and caring for their personal lot.
The duty held the peace kept; lead many to a church house plot.
So as we sit in our homes of comfort with our domestic plans.
Remember this corps as we call to God with praying hands.

AIR FORCE

Flying high and strong in the sky blue.
Over seeing this land of the brave and true.
Serving all with the sight of an eagle.
To strike fear in the heart of all evil,
To soar on high on the breath of our God,
In his favor to serve as his mighty and powerful rod!
To serve with distinction and humble demure!
Their lives they give, no thought of fear, in faith pure.
Eyes skyward to the throne of the one on high,
These men and women of blue fight with their righteous cry!
For their safety and service to this country, may we pray!
That God will watch over them now and every day.

Written for Ruth Marie Stogner to make her day and bring her smiles each time she reads this poem. May she know and feel God's love. Knowing he is always there and will always be there.

DAWN

Dawn is the earliest part of the day.
Dawn is the brightest part of the day.
Dawn is the coolest part of the day.
Dawn is the stillest part of the day.
Dawn is the dewiest part of the day.
Dawn is the freshest part of the day.
Dawn is the sweetest part of the day.
Dawn is the sleepiest part of the day.
Dawn is the prettiest part of the day.
Dawn defies description yet any description is right.
I can compare you to the dawn and I would be right.
Like the dawn God made you. He is never wrong.
Smile you are some of His best handy work.

Charles M. Day III
The Transplanted Mississippian

~(*)~

I received a little good news today, 03-28-06; "DAWN" Has won from the International Library of Poetry, (through poetry.com) the "<u>EDITORS CHOICE AWARD</u>". OK Ruth Marie you're famous. Enjoy
Charles

I am now sitting at the computer compiling the words I have said in poetry and prose over the last few years. I look back to see what I have been saying and find that I have been showing that there is unmistakable poof that God was, is and will always be here. That God need nothing form us but instead we need everything from him. And for us to have all that we need, all we need to do is give true fulfilling love to one another, which in turn gives love to God. That is why God sent his son Jesus Christ as a sacrifice for us. This act of pure love from God shows his depth of feeling for us. What other proof do we need!

PROOF

The sky, blue and bright or filled with clouds is proof.
A might oak with knurled bark and full leafy head is proof.
The birds that nest there with their bright colors and tunes of silver is proof
 A gurgling creek in a forest dale is proof.
The fish that swim and bull frog that croaks there, is proof.
 A mighty river strong and wide is proof.
The currents there in, pushing strong to the Gulf is proof.
The purple oceans so deep and big with curling waves and foamy tips are proof.
The Whales and sharks and all the teaming life that abound there is proof.
The view of earth so blue and bright is proof.
The moon and the stars and the beautiful magnificence of its spatial expanse are proof.
But as I watch you grow up from a babe in my arms through your child hood into the young and beautiful lady you will become. And when I look into your eyes I know and see and feel the proof.
The proof through a gift that was given to me in you, I see that there is a GOD in heaven and I know that he is there for you and me and all.
Oh my child may it be that you see all that I have seen and know and see the **PROOF!**

My daughter, **Anna Charmayne**; She is all I need as proof.

Explanation to my children about clicks

THE CIRCLE

Inside the circle is warm and friendly.
Outside the circle is cold and frosty.
Inside the circle there is fun and happiness.
Outside the circle is sad and cruel.
Inside the circle is where the "in crowd" is.
Outside the circle is where everyone else is.
Inside the circle mistakes are never made.
Outside the circle is where all the mistakes are made.
Inside the circle everyone is tongue and cheek.
Outside the circle no one knows anything for sure.
Inside the circle those that know keep it for themselves.
Outside the circle are those that don't know and will never know.
Inside the circle, it is all smoke and mirrors.
Outside the circle are those that look in and are dazzled.
Only one circle is worthy to be inside of is,
 God the father, Christ the son, and the Holy Spirit.
When the human circle hurts. The circle of the Trinity heals.
May the Circle of the Trinity be the circle you are in!

~(*)~

AMERICA

America is said to be unforgiving.
America has forgiven more debt than any other country.
America is said to be unfeeling.
America has been there "first" whenever a friendly hand was needed.
America is said to be cheap.
America has given more money in aid in times of disaster than any other country.
America?? What is America?
America is where most of the people have hearts or gold and a spirit of silver
America is the country that lives the dream that others are afraid and refuse to live.
America is the country that was given Truth, Justus and Honor that it may share with all who ask.
America, for this is why, you are denounced, refused and sold out.
America, remember September 11th 2001. All other dates pale in comparison to the evil done that day.
America, remember this date, for on this date you were stabbed in the back by a **<u>COWARD</u>**.

A Point made by
Charles M. Day III
The transplanted Mississippian

~(*)~

I sent two care packages to Major Ray Causey and Specialist Suzanne Gordy. They are members of my Church. I also sent this poem. I hope and pray the many have read it and knelt to the Lord God.

I KNEEL AND I PRAY

I kneel and I pray that I walk the way the Lord my God has walked.
I kneel and I pray that I speak in the way the lord my God speaks.
I kneel and I pray that I will see the way the Lord my God sees.
I kneel and I pray that I feel the way the Lord my God Feels.
I kneel and I pray that I will wake every day and seek the face of the Lord my God.
I kneel and I pray that I will sleep and dream I am sitting at the feet of the Lord my God.
I kneel and I pray that I go home with the mind that the Lord my God wants me to have.
I kneel and I pray that I will live in the sacrificed life the lord my God has lived.
I kneel and I pray that if needed I will die in the light of the lord My God.

An unknown US soldier praying in Iraq. Giving God Thanks

~(*)~

Poetry is a cleansing of the mind in order to focus on a task at hand. I is also a stretching of one's soul to the outer limits of ability. It is also just plain fun some times.

SHE SHOUTS

She shouts! No one hears me.
She shouts! I call in vain.
She shouts! If only someone would listen.
She shouts! I have the truth, the way.
She shouts! I have the answer will you not turn my way?
She shouts! I have seen it before, I do know why.
She walks away. She is wisdom, and no-one cares.
She cries woefully. Who will listen, who will understand?
   "For her proceeds are better than the profits of silver, and her gain, better than fine gold. She is more precious than fine rubies, and all the things you may desire cannot compare with her." Prov. 3:14&15

An Enduring truth from
Charles M. Day III
The Transplanted Mississippian

The following poem was written to my Wife for her birthday in April of 2003. In December that same year, "Wife Noble", won the International library of poetry's "Editors Choice ward"

**EDITOR'S CHOICE AWARD
DECEMBER 2003**

"WIFE NOBLE"

My Life is complete- I have a
Wife noble!
When I am mad- I have a
Wife Noble!
When I am frustrated and cannot think- I have a
Wife Noble!
When the brightness of the day is dull in my eyes- I have a
Wife Noble!
When the children are too much and silence is a must- I have a
Wife Noble!
When I disagree with her and I know she is wrong- I have a
Wife Noble!
When the day is done and the pain and aches are on me- I have a
Wife Noble!
When I lay in the bed and need a touch- I have a
Wife Noble!
When I fall to my Knees and pray to God.
I thank him for giving me a
Wife Noble!

A Phrase of Joy from
Charles M. Day III
The Transplanted Mississippian

My one and only, "WIFE NOBLE" God be phrased!

Friday 11-21-03

      This is a letter that I wrote to my church leadership about something that could tear our church apart. Backbiting is a serious offence and should not be allowed to get out of hand. Yet in this case the Backbiters won by default. A sad case, that caused the needless loss of good people. And other wise good church made a bad error. Only God can now pull any good from the leavings.

      I don't always pay attention to the grapevine. Yet this story is too good to let alone. I maybe shaking a hornets' nest into frenzy but I feel I must say something. I can accept the stinging I will receive because of my words.

      It has come to my attention that a few of our members have insulted a member of our church. It seems that Don Martin has been asked to teach the singles class. Three members of the singles department have threatened to leave the church if he is brought on board as teacher. Then they had sworn the interim singles pastor to silence. This is not biblical or right. Every man or woman has the God given right to face his or her accusers and no man may tie the pastor's hands. The pastor must stand for truth and be allowed to speak when God tells him to. Anonymity is not a good thing in this case.

      These three people are acting like cowards. If they will not face Don and allow the air to be cleared between them, then as far as I am concerned <u>they can leave</u>. I don't want cowards among us! A Coward will only cause damage to the church and must be taught a way out of cowardice or turned out all together. I don't like the ladder.

      Don is a very good man and a loyal servant of God. Don is worthy and must be allowed to serve God the way God want him to serve. Believe me I have seen God's work in my life and see it still in the lives of others. I promise you this, I am a fighter and if allowed I will fight for Don's rights in this church because it is righteous to do so.

      The truth always cuts clean and lets the wounds heal better/

THE TRUTH IS

There are those that talk behind the backs of others and hide their faces not to be known.
THE TRUTH IS. God knows the hearts of all men and takes note of them.
There are men that have lungs like daggers and forked tongs as they speak.
THE TRUTH IS. God know the words of men and uses then all for his good.
There are men that walk a crooked line so that they can dodge in and out.
THE TRUTH IS. God knows the path of men and weaves them as he wants.
There are men who want the world to be as they see it.
THE TRUTH IS. God's sight goes beyond the sight of men.
There are men that want the world to say what they say.
THE TRUTH IS. God's word made the world and all things on it.
There are men that want the world to feel what they feel.
THE TRUTH IS. God' feelings were shown in Christ.
There are men who want the world to love all the ways of all men and condemn none.
THE TRUTH IS. God's love was given with Christ. God love is not the way of men.
There are men who claim they have the truth, know the way and show the light.
THE TRUTH IS, God's son "Christ Jesus "is the truth, the way and the light.
There are men that say that the path to God is by them.
THE TRUTH IS, God's path is only through Christ Jesus his son.
THE TRUTH IS, we should act on GOD wills.
THE TRUTH IS, God's will is sought through prayer and diligence in his **precepts**.

                    A thought from
                    Charles M. Day III
                The Transplanted Mississippian

~(*)~

You can always tell the deferent's between people by their attitudes and the way each handle stress and strain.

HE THAT DOES, HE THAT DOES NOT

He that does, walk a true line and strays not!
He that does not wanders and has no path.
He that does, Talks with words that are under stood.
He that does not speaks and says nothing.
He that does shows the facts and the proof as they stand.
He that does not confuses the issues and dumbfounds the facts.
He that does is Just. Honest and Honorable. He will hold these things equal for all.
He that does not is not just, has no honesty and will not be honorable.
He that does sees himself as a helper, a mender and helper to all.
He that does not vainly sees himself as a leader a man of the people, a strong defender and is not.
Which are you? How do you see yourself?
"I all your ways acknowledge Him, and he will direct your path. Do not be wise in your own eyes; Fear the Lord and depart from evil. Prov. 3:6&7

A Thought of
Charles M. Day III
The Transplanted Mississippian

~(*)~

11-03-03

Mr. President

Today I have been getting calls for work. The prayers of my friends are coming through and the hand of God in moving in my direction. As much as you or I want to push ahead and deal with the day-to-day problems, without God's help we can do very little. Forever step we take on our own it seems that we stumble back two or three. Let me predict that we will be successful with God's help. I can see in the not too distant future that Saddam Hussein and Osama Ben Laden will be caught. There will be a tip that on of our solders will act on quickly that will cause this to happen. And I feel that each of the captures will not be to far apart in time. I feel this way because, I pray to God that it happens quickly in God's time. So That he may show us and the world that He is truly in charge not us.

WHO IS IN CHARGE

A child falls and skins his knee.
Who is in charge!
A car skids and crashes.
Who is in charge!
A sparrow falls from the sky.
Who is in charge!
In pain a woman give birth.
 Who is in charge!
With the last cast, of a no catch day an angler catches a trophy bass.
Who is in charge!
A doctor finds that one bleeder in a tangled mass that no one could find.
Who is in charge!
 A fireman finds that one lost child in a smoking building in the nick of time.
 Who is in charge!
A stranger saves a drowning person then walks away before he is thanked. Who is in charge!
Look around at all that is happening and see.
Who is in charge?
From the smallest to the largest occurrence,
 Who is in Charge?
The LORD GOD is in charge! That's <u>WHO</u>!

Charles M. Day III
The Transplanted Mississippian

~(*)~

I watched my son this afternoon and these words came rolling out. Thank you, God, for my son.

MY SON

Blond hair, blue-green eyes with his sand pale, has the world by
a puppy-dogs tail.
Three feet tall and is a giant to all he sees below him.
No frog, lizard, cricket, or bug can escape him.
Running barefoot here there and everywhere!
Shirt wrong side out, right side out or no shirt at all.
He runs and plays in his long, long days.
He fall and he cries, It's a great big surprise. Then he does it again.
He stops and surveys all, and finds this world is his big red ball.
Back I see when it was me and then in him I do see me.
So long ago it was, when I was where he is.
Then him I watch and see and make believe he is me.
I smile as he wonders at the bird in the tree.
I laugh as he prods a toad with a stick to make a trick.
I remember me as he puffs the seed of a dandy lion.
My son is a gift given by God late in life of his blessing for me to see.
That he is a blessing and a chore for me to see.
O my God I do praise thee for giving him to me.
I do praise thee for letting me see me in him and him in me.
And when it is time, that he sees as I see.
His son in him and him in his son.

A father's prayer from
Charles M. Day III
The Transplanted Mississippian

11-01-03

Mr. President;

I have, a 4 year old, son named Sterling. My wife takes him to a mother's morning out program at our church on Tuesdays. One Tuesday my wife took him and as they arrived Sterling raised his hand and shouted "hello kids I'm back." Now the children that were playing there were a little older than him and they did not know Sterling. But to him it did not seem to matter. He was glad to be there this was his school and he liked it.

Christ said that, "we can't enter the gates of heaven unless we have the innocents of a child". How do we regain this type of "innocents". As far as I see we never lose it. It just fades back in our personality every day we contend with this day-today world of ours. These innocents, surfaces from time to time when we make an honest mistake or stumble into a situation we know nothing about. The clueless feeling we have is in fact our innocents. The more we work with this world the less we notice our innocents. We can't call it up when we want it but it is always there when we stumble. Yet we need it to get into heaven. How do we get it? What is the key?

The key is our lord Jesus Christ. The simple act of accepting him as our savior opens the door. Our effort to follow his teachings and to do our day-to-day tasks in the manor he would do them. This brings our innocents closer to the surface. The more we follow Christ the more access we have to our innocents, until that day when we, really do need it. Then we can call our innocents at will.

How amazing and simple the answer is. We find our innocents and call it at will, all because we follow one who gave his life for us. And in return we follow him because the path he trod he made for us. Our innocents, is actually Jesus Christ living in us. We are him and he is us. How sweet, how simple, how so, so right it is.

To his sweet, sweet voice we then begin to hear.

I HEAR

I scurry from here to there and all around. I hear someone say "slow down."
I talk fast, speak smoothly and choose the right words. I hear someone say "be Quite my child let me speak."
I eat my food quickly I am in a hurry. I hear someone say "I have food for your soul, eat and enjoy.
I move so fast I don't know where to go. I hear someone say "Come with me I know where to go."
I hear people say do this not that, stop here, go there. Then I hear someone say"Listen to me I won't fail you."
I am so tired yet I cannot rest. I hear someone say "Lay here; I give you peace and rest."
I wake worried and wonder what to do next. I hear someone say. "Place your worries on me I know what to do."
I now know the answer. When I HEAR that voice I will obey and I will worry and scurry no more.

A Thought of
Charles M. Day III
The Transplanted Mississippian

~(*)~

10-27-03

Mr. President;

OK, something is not right in Baghdad. We have suicide bombers killing anybody and everybody. You have a bomber that you caught who is from Syria. You don't want to say anything confirming support for terrorism from this country or any other country that are or that may be allowing human bombers into Iraq. What gives? One of our greatest presidents was a very good peacemaker. Yet he would fight when necessary. His name was Teddy Roosevelt. His motto was "Speak softly but carry a big stick."

I think that you should speak softly to the Syrian government and any other government who is involved. Speak softly yet in a very firm voice, "control the zealots in your country or we will control them for you."

I do not like war and I do not like killing people. The problem is that the Middle Eastern zealot does not have the same feelings. They do not care who they kill as long as they get their way. There should be no doubt the Middle Eastern zealot is out to convert the entire world one country at a time. Don't let anyone tell you different. You cannot get the idea across to a Zealot that he is better off if he lives with people who have different ideas. In his mind his way is the only way and he will die to make sure that everybody thinks his way. I say let him die if he wants to just let us decide when and where not the zealot.

`What I have said may be seen as a little harsh but "YOU DON'T PET A RABID DOG. YOU KILL IT." If the rabid dog can be saved you save it. But if you can't save the dog you kill it and don't waste time. It says in Ecclesiastes 3:1-8;

"There is a time to be born and a time to die, A time to plant and a time to uproot, A time to kill and a time to heal. A time to tear down and a time to build, a time to weep and a time to laugh. A time to morn and a time to dance, A time to scatter stones and a time to gather them up. A time to keep and a time to through away, A time to tear and a time to mend. A time to be silent and a time to speak, A time to love and a time to hate. A time for war and a time for peace."

Sir, It is time to stop the nonsense. You must "NAME A SPADE A SPADE AND DON'T TIP TOE THROUGH THE TULIPS WHILE DOING IT." GET IT DONE

GET IT DONE

If some needs a coat, give him one. Get it done.
If a man needs work help him find some. Get it done.
If someone is hurt, help him. Get it done.
If someone is thirsty, give him some water. Get it done.
If someone is hungry! Feed him. Get it done.
If a child need spanked, do it. Get it done.
If someone attacks you! Fight back to win! Get it done.
If they want to make real peace, go with them and do it. Get it done.
Whatever you do, do it from real strength and character and
GET IT DONE

A Concerned Thought of
Charles M. Day III
The Transplanted Mississippian

10-29-03

Mr. President;

      Today I mowed the grass. Ok, that is not much of anything. But when you think about it, a lot has been done. You see the grass is therapeutic. I have an acre to mow. This is time that I can concentrate on one thing and let my mind relax. Then when I am finished I am better able to cope with day-to-day life. This is what God wants us to do. Relax our minds and let the world alone for a little while. Christ got away many times with his disciples to be alone and pray. To focus on what is important, His relationship with God and his disciples.

      I watch you on TV and read about you in the news. As busy as you are I wonder if you are getting proper down time. I personally don't want you to burn out your candle at both ends. The United Nations is giving you some trouble even though on the surface they look like they are helping. Their help in on again off again. This is why down time is important. Time alone, just you and God. Afterwards the world is a tame kitty cat.

      My wife says that you never get these e-mails and that I am wasting my time. I say that even if you are not seeing any of them someone is and they are getting the benefit of what I write. God will put the e-mail in the proper hands. I hope you see some of them.

TIME

Time, time there is never enough.
Time to sleep, time to work, time to study and time to a breath.
Where does all the time go.
Time to drive, time to read time to study and time to live.
How much time is left?
Time to rush here and time to rush there. Is there enough time?
Time to pray. I must have more time.
Time to commune with God and time to speak with my savior.
Time to ease my mind, time to take in God's word.
Time to do God's will.
God's time.

A prayer from
Charles M. Day III
The Transplanted Mississippian
~(*)~

63

10-26-03

President Bush;

    As I was reading the Bible, looking for something to calm my nerves and fears from the day- to- day stress. I came across 27th Psalm and through of you. I have been watching you through the news and the stress on you must be almost unbearable. After reading this Psalm my fears began to ease.

"The lord is my light and my salvation, WHOM SHALL I FEAR? When evil men begin to advance against me to devour my flesh. when my enemies and my foes attack me, THEY STUMBLE AND FALL. Though an army besieges me, MY HEART WILL NOT FEAR, though a war broke out against me, EVEN THEN I WILL BE COMFIDENT."

How can I take this and apply it to me. The next verse answered that. "One thing that I ask Lord, this is what I seek: THAT I MAY DWELL IN THE HOUSE OF THE LORD ALL THE DAYS OF MY LIFE. To gaze upon the beauty of the Lord and to seek him in his temple, FOR IN THE DAYS OF TROUBLE HE WILL KEEP ME SAFE IN HIS DWELLING. He will hide me in the shelter of his tabernacle and set me high upon a rock. THEN MY HEAD WILL BE EXALTED ABOVE THE ENEMIES WHO SURROUND ME; At His tabernacle will I sacrifice with shouts of joy; I will sing and make music to the lord."

    I hope that this will somehow give you strength as you go through this and your next term in office. I pray to God that he gives you another term in office for the sake of this country. Mr. President I have a new computer and a new email address. But you will recognize my poetry. I hope this two will give you comfort and strength.

MY EYES HAVE SEEN

My eyes have seen the richness and the lean of this land.
My eves have seen the praise worthy and the fool hearty of this land.
My eyes have seen the heroes and the villains of this land.
My eyes have seen the great houses and the hovels of this land.
My eyes have seen the great, the honorable and the low down, disdained deeds of this land.
My eyes have seen what great men and what infamous men can do to this land.
My eyes have seen the cries of praise and the cries of woe in this land.
My eyes have seen the love and the hate in this land.
My eyes have seen, my eyes have seen much in this land.
My eyes have seen all things and more in this land.
I my eyes wait to see the joy on the return of the Lord Jesus Christ to this land.
My eyes will see, one day soon, the end of all that is evil in this land.
May your eyes see the same, in this land!

A Thought of
Charles M. Day III
The Transplanted Mississippian

SUNDAY 10-19-03

Mr. President;

I went to church today and Pastor Mark taught a sermon on tithing. This is the first, in a three part series of sermons. All the sermons I heard today (radio, TV, Ect.) were on the proper use of money. What it boils down to is this, <u>WE</u> in this Country have moved into a period of growth in building our own personal wealth at the cost of our souls. We are so obsessed with keeping up with or besting our neighbors that we forget why we are here.

We are here to advance God's kingdom, period. The wealth we get, we are to use to that end, I.e., build God's kingdom. The money comes from God anyway, (I realize that there are some that think this Idea is dumb and wrong.) If a person uses his money wisely to advance God's kingdom, the money won't run out, The proof is out there to see, this way only increases the worth of a person in God's eye as well as in the eyes of other people. Yet there is the Humanist point of view that says that we are here for our own good and the heck with anyone else. How blind can the humanist point of view get! Sir, if anyone listens to that babble and follows it the path of destruction is not far away. OK, let's give them one thing. They are willing to push this idea into anyone's face until the upcoming generation is willing to believe this fallacy is true. Say it enough and people will start to believe it.

Is it not written, "For the foolishness of God is wiser than mans wisdom and the weakness of God is stronger than mans strength. Cor.1:25. These pearls of wisdom are lost on the humanist. I only hope that the advice that you get is from God's word or Christian founded and based friends.

I read that more US soldiers were killed in Iraq today. I feel that someone should be voicing the Goodness of our presence there. Maybe the US should put a ship off the coast of Iraq and put a fully functioning TV station on it and beam the full truth to the people of Iraq. This radio station we control, using an Iraqi announcer and news crew. They report to the people of Iraq what is really happening in their country and around the world. Counter any negative newscast by other broadcasters shortly after they give their view. No military people in view on the station, everyone wearing civvies. I have one question. Where is our heart?

WHERE THE HEART IS

Men grab and scrap for every dime and hold it close. Where is our heart?
The pride is in what we can have and what is kept. Where is our heart?
Pride in the accomplishments we make. Where is our heart?
We point to the glory of mankind and his great future. Where is our heart?
With fanfare we advance knowledge. Where is our heart?
We revel in our wisdom. Where is our heart?
We buy more and consume more. Where is our heart?
All we do is to the greater glory of man. Where is our heart?
We had better know where our heart is or we will fall.
For where your treasure is, there your heart will be also. Luke 12:34
Where our heart should be is. "I have sought your face with all my heart;
Be gracious to me according to your promise. Ps 119:58

A Thought from
Charles M. Day III
The Transplanted Mississippian

~(*)~

Mr. President;

      I am a little ticked at some people in congress. There is a bill that will be on your desk to be signed by you and I am glad to hear that you will sign it. I applaud you loudly. However there are a few senators and representatives that are lining up to have the law declared Unconstitutional. This is the ban on Partial Birth Abortion.

      What I am about to say will not be heard in a favorable light by these people. If you wish to quote me you may. But I must say It. According to the AMA" there is no medical reason or Necessity to do Partial Birth Abortion." The only reason that this procedure is done is for money. The child that is being aborted can live outside of the mother without artificial help. Because of this very point this little body is the perfect research tool. This is where the money angle comes into play. Not only is the doctor paid for this procedure but the doctor turns around and sells the body parts to research companies in or out of the USA. Each of the little bodies can bring a minimum or 25,000 to $30,000 into the doctors business or into the Doctors pocket form such sales. If you multiply this dollar amount by the number of procedures he will do in one year, let say a conservative no.# like 50, This means he will generate a total payday of $1,500,000 to placate his **$$GREED$$**. Worst-case scenario is the mother and the doctor are profiting from the death of the child. It is illegal in this country to do this. Yet it is being done. There are several web sites on the net (most are out of this country) that are begging for these little bodies.

      The Senators, Representatives and Judges that support this procedure and wish to make it legal along with the Doctors and nurses that perform the procedure and guilty of MURDER IN THE FIRST DEGREE. Christ, himself said, " Heaven is made up of such as the little children Mark 10:17 and It would be better that a man put a mill stone on his shoulder and cast himself into the sea than to cause one of these to sin." What is God's punishment for taking a child's life? There is an old adage that says "if it has feathers like as duck, if it waddles like a duck, and looks like a duck is has got to be a duck.

      So if a human egg and human sperm join and begin to grow, at the minuet it happens it is a human. It does not matter if it is two cells or four cells or eight cells or fully developed in the womb it is still a human being.

      Mr. President in your next statement of the union address or the fan fare that surrounds this bill, you need of state the seriousness of this procedure. That if any doctor uses the clause " for the health of the mother" to perform this inhumane procedure, He is in violation of the law. If that clause is in the bill please line item it out.

LIFE

To start it takes two.
To nurture it takes effort and pain.
To watch it grow takes tinder-loving care.
To watch it spread its wings and fly is pleasure.
To destroy it is mad.
To destroy it before it has a chance to live is sinful madness.
To gloat and profit from it is a waste of humanity and death to us all.
Its life is worth all pain, all hurt, all ill will.
Its little life was planned by God and God is not amused!
Beware! He who takes human life for granted!
For THE LORD OUR GOD is watching closely.

A Thought of
Charles M. Day III
The Transplanted Mississippian

What is Life?

This is Life and it is hard to beat. This is Anna Charmayne at 15 days old and me reborn at 43 years of age.

Charles M. Day III
The Transplanted Mississippian

~(*)~

11-26-03

The pilgrims were starving and near the end of their ropes. The spring was just starting and they turned to God for direction. God sent a group of Native Americans to teach them what native plants in this new world were good to eat. They also introduced them to Maze and taught them to grow it. At the end of the first harvest on American soil, the pilgrims sat down with their new Native American friends and thanked God.

The holiday we celebrate today is to thank God for his grace and the abundance God has given us, as He did the Pilgrims. God has given us the abundance we have. Yet we are being bombarded with anti-God propaganda. More and more we have stopped believing in God's Grace each day. If we look closely at our past we will see the truth. (The ant-God and revisionist forces are trying to obscure the evidence and hide it from us.)

It was God that granted us our position in this world today. It is God that blessed our efforts in the past that allowed us to reach our position in the world today. It will be God that takes it away if we do not realize who holds the true rains of power. I know of the efforts of the anti-God people and there efforts to rewrite history. I also know that we the people can over ride them. They know this to be true because we out number them. We have the right to keep our leadership torch in this world. But we have to recognize that we can't do it without God's blessing. We must stand and complain about those that are forcing change that will lead us away from the absolute truth. Yes, there is an absolute truth We Christens know it and we must shout it as loud as the detractors shout there lies. If not, WE LOSE FOREVER.

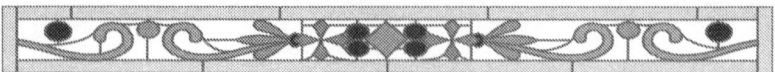

THANKS

Thank some who helps you. It will come back to you.
 Thank a friend for his advice whether or not he takes it. It will come back to you.
Thank the person that gives you a dollar. It will come back to you.
Thank your mate for the kiss she gave you. It will come back to you.
Thank your teacher for his or her work. It will come back to you.
Thank any one that works hard at their Job. It will come back to you.
Thank GOD for his love and Grace.
IT WILL COME BACK TO YOU.

Special thanks, to the men that went before us. They are always with us.

A Prayer from
Charles M. Day III
The Transplanted Mississippian

~(*)~

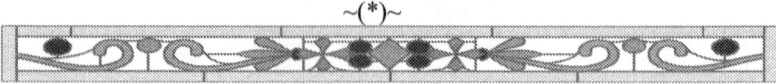

10-23-03

Mr. President:

Well today is the stepping-stone of oop's. I made a mathematical error. Honest, I did not know it was rubber. I got in the mail the dreaded insufficient funds Letter. I quickly looked at my checkbook and poured over the figures. The old, I subtracted it wrong, syndrome. Ooah, it just cost $20 dollars. Fortunately the bank paid the check. There is a lesson in this somewhere and the glory belongs to God.

Now, I know that it sounds like I have lost it by saying that. However, let's look at this from another point of view. God does not cause bad things to happen to us. Instead God does allow bad to happen to us in order to A. prepare us for something that we do not see now. B. Stop us from doing something that we should not do. C. Change our direction in life.

If we ignore these red flags we will continue to dig the hole we are in deeper and deeper and deeper until we can't see daylight. Well when I was a small boy there was a rule we had to follow when we crossed the street. You had to stop look and listen for oncoming cars and trucks.

When God puts up a red flag, Stop and assess where you are at that point in your life. Look for anything that may be out of place, missing or something that you are not quite seeing. Listen to relevant advice on that subject from people you trust and are educated about that subject.

Now this may seem like I am blowing up a simple but painful incident as an act of God. But in my short 53 years of life I have stumbled, fumbled and fallen to many times to see this as anything but a red flag. As of yet I do not know what it is but I have stopped and I am looking, and I will listen.

STOP LOOK AND LISTEN

A mocking bird sings in the tree. Stop, look and listen.
The wind blows gently through the tree. Stop, look and listen.
The leaves rustle as the winds blows. Stop, look and listen.
The bird flutters as the wind blows through its feathers. Stop look and listen.
The air is fragrant as it blows. Stop, look and listen.
The temperature is pleasant and cool. Stop look and listen.
The large limb cracks and falls. Stop, look and listen.
The limb crashes to the ground. Stop, look and listen.
You walk on in safety. Aren't you glad you stopped, looked and listened?

A Thought from
Charles M. Day III
The transplanted Mississippian

~(*)~

Do you see the fallen limb?????

10-?-03

Mr. President:

    To day had been very slow. The month has so far, been dismal. I own a small company. My company does Tree service work, installs roofing systems and landscaping. Nothing has come in and I have bills to pay. You can say that this month has been very bad. I look at you position in the white house as leader of this country and see my little problems as not so big.

    With all the problems I have I can sit back and count my Blessings. I have a roof over my head, clothes on my back and my health, (even though my feet hurt and my back aches and from time to time my head aches unlike any). I have a loving 10 years old, a rambunctious 4 year old and a wife that was given to me by divine declaration, (She is an angle most of the time and a little less some of the time. One day if you want to know I will tell you why.

    I wonder why I have these things, even though it is said never look and gift horse in the mouth. I have often asked, why has God placed me here? My Pastor is doing a sermon about that very question. The Pastor says we are to serve God and worship him. We must serve him in each of our ways in whatever we are doing. We should ask what would or how would Christ handle our lives. The answer is expressed in Psalm 33:4 &5. "For the word of the Lord is right and true and he is full of his unfailing love."

    God wants each of us to do everything we do to praise him. We glorify his mane every time we seek after the right way in doing things, in honor and justice with no malice or evil intent. We must glorify his mane ever time we do our jobs and give back while doing it . We must glorify God in everything we in our lives. Every thought, every action we must Glorify God. We will fail many times in our lives but every time we succeed it is made easier for us the next time we put forth the effort. If we keep trying we will succeed more than we fail.

    My daughter asked me to tell you that you are doing a good jab as President. If a 10 year old who does not know or understand what is really going on around her in this world can say that, "You are doing a good job."
I know that God's hand is on you. Please do all that you can do, the way that God would have you do it! Please don't be like King Saul in the Old Testament and believe that you know better than God.

I ENDEAVOR TO SEEK HIS WILL

I endeavor to seek his will when I get up in the morning.
I endeavor to seek his will when I pray.
I endeavor to seek his will as I drive my car.
I endeavor to seek his will as I climb the tree or nail the nail or rake the grass.
I endeavor the seek his will as I breath the air or feel the breeze on my face.
I endeavor to do his will as I correct my children.
I endeavor to do his will as I kneel to pray at night.
I endeavor to do his will as I kiss my wife.
I endeavor to do his will as I sleep at night.
I endeavor to do his will regardless of what I do.
O my God may I always, always, always ENDEAVOR TO DO YOU WILL

A Thought of
Charles M. Day III
The Transplanted Mississippian

~(*)~

A hole in the clouds, a brake in the weather, reprieve from the storm!
The results of seeking God's will is like this.

Mr. President;

I look at this world and know that you have done the right things so far. You have brought to a head the terrorist problem and the rest of the world is not seeing the truth. Sir, you are a wise man to this point. Now I think you need a new perspective in Iraq and in Afghanistan. I feel you need to show a more aggressive resolve and jump in and think Legal outside box for a while. Start to use the Terrorist M.O. against the Terrorist.

1. Our trucks don't go anywhere that command does not know whom, where and why and the number in the group.

2. A larger Iraqi US underground must be used.

3. More check points must be set up in and around buildings.

4. There is a tunnel being use to smuggle weapons in Baghdad. Find it and use the tunnel against the insurgents.

5. This may be harsh but all Syrian and Iranian citizen must be expelled from Iraq no exceptions. Even close down their Embassies if they do not help.

6. feed the children and teens good holism food. If you see a woman holding a baby, give the mother milk for the child. Don't send a man it will insult the people and the husband. If an elderly man is walking and is in pain, Take him to the doctor then take him to his destination with medicine and food. Basically, feed the hungry and treat the sick. Help the lame to walk, aid the blind in any way possible. See to it that the schools have books to read and study with. Ask if one of the solders can teach in one of the school form time to time. When this happens bring some candy and fruit.

7. In the cities and towns where they still have an enemy presents, show up with a truck or two loaded with food and fresh water and passes it out to the people. Say to them that we are there friends and say thank you to them. Then just leave. Some of this food will fall into the hands of the insurgents, SO WHAT OF IT. The majority of the food will get to the people and show that we are not the bad guys. Do this enough and we will be out of there faster and stabilize the region at the same time.

HAND WRITEING ON THE WALL

In a time long ago a large hand appeared and wrote words on a king's wall.
No one could tell the king its meaning.
No one could explain to the King the language of the script.
No one knew what to tell the king.
Then someone remembered an old man that did serve the King's great Grandfather.
He knew that Daniel could read the message. The King called for him.
Daniel looked at the message. Then he looked at the king and said.
"IT IS DONE!"
And that kingdom fell.
It is time for our wise men to read the handwriting on the wall.
If they can!!!

Charles M. Day III
The Transplanted Mississippian

~(*)~

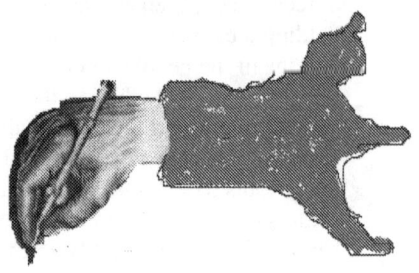

01-04-04

Mr. President;

There are several points that the debates between the democrat contenders brought out. One is the tax cut that you began in this term. Please be specific with your answers. Most people can see through a general statement and find what, if anything to support it.
1. What percentage of the population did the tax cuts effect.
2. How many of those fell into the $20,000 to $50,000 range? And I don't just mean the marriage penalty tax.
3. Did the tax cuts include the people and companies that make $250,000 to 3,000,000 of better?
4. How can you make clear to the democrats about Iraq as to Justification? I think that you should confront Dr. Dean and shut him down once and for good. And please be quick about it because some people (not me) think that you are not willing to set him straight, or afraid to.

A statement was made by Rep. Dennis Kucinich that most of the larger corporations, (drug and insurance), pay the CEO's and members of the board of directors 2 & 3 million per year. He read from what is supposed to be facts and figures in his position. I realized that research must be done and it is not cheap, but that kind of paycheck is over doing it if true.
5. Is this truth, and what can we do to see that this is changed.

These questions are just a few of the many there are. But these and other questions must be answered and in a loud and clear manor. Hear my words sir.

HERE MY WORDS

Do I speak with double talk!
Hear my words.
Do I talk the talk and walk the walk.
Hear my words.
Do I speak with dizzy facts and figures that overwhelm the mind?
 Hear my words.
Do I speak one way here and another way there!
 Here my words.
Do I hide my life then say my peace.
Hear my words.
Do I speak and peak and speak and speak and speak and say nothing.
Hear my words.
Do I lie and say it is the truth so help me G===.
Hear my words.
Do I use the truth only when it suits me!
Hear my words.
Do you really hear, do you care to heart!
Who so ever keeps his word, in him is the love perfected. 1 JN 2:5

A Though from
Charles M Day III
The Transplanted Mississippian

~(*)~

A young man was standing on the sidewalk by a public school with a Bible in his hand. He was on the sidewalk sharing the gospel with anyone who listens. He was in a group of several doing the same thing. This young man had stepped off the sidewalk to pick up something that had rolled away from the group. He was then arrested for teaching the Bible on school grounds. If he had stayed on the sidewalk he would have not been arrested. Absurd is it not. The following was written because of this incident. May God have mercy on us all! And may I add the Judge that sentenced him should have been horse whipped for her scathing remarks, which made no sense.

SPEECH

Speech; the freedom there of, does not Exist in the U.S. anymore.
Speech; the freedom there of, has been replaced with political correctness.
Speech, the freedom there of, to speak the truth the whole truth, cannot be done any more.
Speech, the freedom there of, is not taught in our schools anymore, because it may offend.
Speech, the freedom there of, can no longer be expressed on a public corner any more.
Speech, the freedom there of, is dead in this country today.
Speech, the freedom there of, we live in a gilded dictatorship.
Speech, the freedom there of, is replaced with edited comments as not to offend.
Speech, the freedom there of, for **WE THE PEOPLE** it must not be allowed to cease

A Thought from
Charles M Day III
The Transplanted Mississippian

This piece of prose was sent to friends and family in 2000 because of the Bible hate I had seen on TV and in the news. May God use these meager words to speak to the hearts of men!

IN THE BEGINNING AND NOW

In the beginning- our Founding Fathers wouldn't make a new country without Gods help.
Now- there are those in our government who are trying and are removing God form our Government.
In the beginning- George Washington wouldn't take the oath of office without a Bible.
Now- the Bible is insulted, ridiculed, look at as an unwanted history and where possible thrown out the window.
In the beginning- this country walked in the light of God, talked with the power of God.
Now- this country walks in its own dim light and talks with own meager power.
In the beginning- God marched with our soldiers and made them strong.
Now- our soldiers march alone. They are ordered to leave God at home.
In the beginning- God grew a hedge around this country and kept it safe.
Now- the hedge is being mowed down and God is being told to stay away.
In the beginning- God and the USA were one and no one would have it any other way.
Now- God is separate from the USA and Christians don't care, won't care or afraid to care.
In the beginning- God was the architect that helped a country become great.
Now- this country has turned its back on God the Architect.
In the beginning- there were men that defended God and Country.
 Now- there is still people that will defend God and Country.
ARE YOU ONE?
In the beginning- Men and Women stood for only truth, God's Truth.
Now- there is still men and women who will stand for the only truth, God's truth.
ARE YOU ONE?

A Thought of truth from a servant of The LORD our God.
Charles M. Day III
The Transplanted Mississippian

~(*)~

06-17-00

E-mailed to the President, as a rebuttal to those feminist, and others, that wishes to take the guiding influence of children from their parents.

CHILDREN

To behold something of beauty and enjoy it is pleasure.
To nurture Growth and watch it blossom is pure joy.
To guide and direct a young life to its full potential is love.
To give help, so a child can enjoy life is a fruitful endeavor.
Others, who don't want parents, to raise their children know this.
This is why we are being bombarded by every trick that will take our minds off our children.
Our children are the future. Our children are the key.
Our children are the way we will succeed.
We cannot enter in the future because we are the present.
The future is in the hands of our children.
Our children should be in our hands.
Who will raise our children? We the parents! Or
 The state!
Our fore fathers knew this. They knew that through the education of our children the future was set.
Our enemies know this well. They will steal the minds of our children.
Our future will then change and the sick values of today will stay in the future.
Our children learn that Darwin is right and the Bible is wrong.
Our children learn that it is ok sometimes to tell a little white lie, if it benefits everyone.
Our children learn that the values of the parents are old fashion and useless in this modern world.
Our children learn that money is power and who has the most money has power.
Our children learn that sex is ok and to have lots of it.
When will we learn the lessons of our fore fathers?
That moral restraint is the best. That law should be based on biblical understanding.
Wake up the wolves are at the door and we may be out of ammunition.

An injured child is being aided and prayed over by a Corpsman of the 101st infantry. Praise God for his presents. May God bless his parents!

Charles M. Day III
The Transplanted Mississippian

~(*)~

I got mad today at Brian Gumble because of his negative attitude toward a Christian man and his defiance of the Boy Scouts on their decision not to admit Gays. I wrote the following and e-mailed it to him, and all his bosses and co news people.

BUMBLE GUMBEL

I wonder who has no respect for other's views, Bumble Gumble.
I wonder who has no tolerance, Bumble Gumble.
I wonder who was caught saying the wrong thing, Bumble Gumble.
I wonder whose mouth should be washed out with soap and dried with hot coals. Bumble Gumble.
I wonder if CBS can see the wrong and make it right, Bumble Gumble.
I wonder who should reread the Constitution and see if not all have the right to free speech. Bumble Gumble.
I wonder if the unemployment line can show you the light, Bumble Gumble.
I wonder if you think that you are wise in your own eye, Bumble Gumble.
I wonder if you know that you should "judge not least ye be judged, Bumble Gumble.
I wonder if you know that you are made strong or made weak by the opinions of others, Bumble Gumble.
Pr.29: 1. A man who remains stiff-necked after many rebukes will suddenly be distorted- without remedy.

From the pen of
Charles M. Day
The Transplanted Mississippian

~(*)~

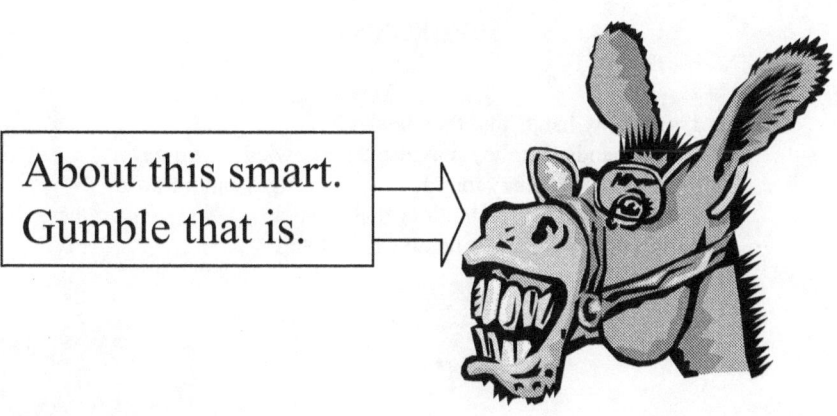

About this smart. Gumble that is.

Another Haiku Poem, again I did not win.

LOVE

Love is all around and is easily found.
It springs from God to flow though all.
It fills the hollowed soul.

~(*)~

I had an operation on my shoulder in 2000 and in 2003. I wrote this prayer for the Doctors that did the Work. This prayer won "Editor's Choice Award" for February 2004

SURGEON'S PRAYER

Lord, guide my hands that they heal.
Steady my hands that they may use the knowledge you gave.
Hold my hands that they may feel your strength and purpose.
Place your hands on my shoulder that I may know that you are there.
All this I ask in your son's name Christ Jesus
Amen

~(*)~

I don't know what caused this prose but it says a lot for so few words.

WORD

I was brought up to say what I mean and mean what I say.
In other words my word is my bond.
I was taught that a hand shake was a contract.
I was taught that a man meets his obligations.
I was taught that a man stands for the truth or dies by his untrue hands.
I was taught the strength one is in the hands of many and the many in the hands of one.
I was taught that there is an absolute and that God is unchanging and is always there.
I was taught that if we stick with Gods unchanging love, that we, in Gods time will succeed.
I was taught- "to first seek Gods will and all these other thing will be added to us.

06-19-2000

This was written in an e-mail to President Bush when his two children were in the news as a negative story. I felt for him that day.

FATHERS

To be one is to know struggle and strife.
To be one is to make tuff decisions.
To be one is to know love and bitterness.
To be one is to know strength and weakness.
To be one is to know the height of ecstasy and the depth of despair.
To be one is to know, God's will for man and to know the joy in the sacrifice that his son Christ made for us.
Oh, the love our Heavenly father has for us.

Penned by
Charles M. Day III
The Transplanted Mississippian

~(*)~

I entered a poetry contest today Called Haiku. The rules were three lines and no more that 21 words from a topic they picked. It must be done in 60 seconds. I did it but did not win. Here is my effort.

REFLECTIONS
Reflections of thought mixing in the mind!
Who am I? What am I?
I am God's child and He loves <u>Me</u>.

60 seconds from
Charles M. Day III
The Transplanted Mississippian

~(*)~

This was written for the first lady, Laura Bush, with honor and respect.
This was written for her, on her first day as the first Lady of the USA.

THE PLACE A STEP BEHIND

There is a place that is a step behind.
It rarely catches up, unless by a fall or design.
It is always there and is always filled.
Filled by some that are qualified and some that are not.
Filled by wives, daughters and friends.
Filled by those that loved and cherished.
Filled by those that seek control.
How and by whom province only knows.
Now, it is your place to fill and hold.
For this man, this office and this country are in your hands.
Fill this place with love and support, honor and truth.
Be strong in God and ask his guidance only.
Myself, The Country and the President your husband,
NEED YOU.

Faith is sometimes a very hard thing to hold onto. Yet without it this world is not a very nice place to be in.

FAITH

Faith is believing, when there is nothing left to believe in.
Faith is believing, that your neighbor will treat you right.
Faith is believing, that your city fathers will not rule against you.
Faith is believing, that your state will not make it hard for you to work.
Faith is believing your country is not trying to undermine your parental rights.
Faith is believing, the Constitution is being kept whole not stripped.
Faith is Believing that our elected officials will not sell us out when elected.
Faith is believing that our country will remain sovereign.
Faith is believing that as Americans we can worship God freely anywhere without being condemned.
Faith is a word that means a lot to us all.
Faith is a word of honor and truth and a word all men can use.
Faith – Faith – Faith say it you might like it.

From the pen of
Charles M. Day III
The Transplanted Mississippian

`~(*)~

This was written to the President of the United States of America on the 1st of May 2006. I then sent it to the Joint chiefs chairman on the 9th of May 2006.

Mr. President:

I think you have forgotten the border patrol in your formula on the question of immigration. These men and women who work on our boarders have been wounded and killed by smugglers of cocaine and illegal aliens. Our boarders are a mess because we have not been diligent as a government in our duty. I know you should rethink your plan. What you have done by making the Illegal, legal, is create a nightmare for the border Patrol and/or the INS. Not all the Illegal aliens will comply, simply because they don't trust in badges of any kind. Plus there are those that have something to hide and the terrorist that want nothing more than to destroy us. Let's face it, if you proceed with the proposed plan. (1) More American Jobs will be lost. (2) Terrorist will get into this country. (3) The officials that control the boarder and get information on illegal aliens will be bogged down in red tape and will not be paid for the extra effort. All in all, sir, with all due respect you have made a bad plan. Please rethink it. The following poem is one of six I wrote that are hanging in the Pentagon.

UNITED STATES BOARDER PATROL

In wooded splendor and desert heat, they keep our boarders safe.
Through the longest day and the endless night,
They watch to stop drug lords and terrorist alike.
No fear is shown as they do their job, though death is close at hand.
Nothing will stop the duty of this fearless band.
Standing with dignity and honor, not caring for their personal lot.
The duty held, the peace kept; lead many to a church house plot.
So as we sit in our homes of comfort with our domestic plans.
Remember this corps as we call to God with praying hands.

A thought from
Charles M. Day III
The Transplanted Mississippian

Mr. President;

       I have heard that Vice-President Chaney will not be able to run another term. If this is true you have a hard choice to make. You need someone that thinks like you as a Christen and yet is strong enough to hold you accountable to the lord God's will. This person has to hold true to all Christen values and help defend the Truth of the Constitution of this country. I don't know where a man like this can be found who is a politician. He must be up to speed on all the national issues or be able to be brought up to speed when chosen. You, do not need someone that will buckle under pressure from one side or the other, or as the axiom says "SPEAK WITH FORKED TUNG". Choose wisely as our Lord and God would have you choose.

THE CHOICE

A hard decision made quickly leads to Error and can make you bleed.
A hard decision made after much thought and much advice will succeed.
To choose in haste will always waste resources and time.
To listen and hear all sides and ideas is to choose wisely and save time.
The choice you must choose is chosen in prayer.
This choice is always right, with insight, if sought day and night.
The choice is yours to choose whether to be in the **deepest dark blues** or in **the light**.
Please always choose to walk with God in all his ways.
It will truly keep all the wolves and dragons away all you days.
SEEK YE FIRST THE COUNCIL OF THE LORD. 1st Kings22: 5
LOOK TO THE LORD AND HIS STRENGTH SEEK HIS FACE ALWAYS.
Ps. 105:4

A Thought from
Charles M. Day III
The Transplanted Mississippian

~(*)~

A Final word and praise Read here and bow your head for those that go ahead to clear the way and make us all safe and free.

It is their **Honor** to have served us, and our **Blessing** they have died for our sakes in that service.

"There is not a gift greater than to give one's life for another"

This is a statement from our Lord Jesus Christ, the only son of GOD, who gave, **"no one took it"**, his life and paid the debt for all of U.S. Phrase be to the lord our God because of the sacrifice of his SON. We give Phrase to our service men and women, who fought and died to keep us safe.

Figure 1-The death of three soldiers in Iraq honored by their comrades at arms. May their sacrifice be, remembered!

www.ingramcontent.com/pod-product-compliance
Lightning Source LLC
Chambersburg PA
CBHW022007100426
42738CB00041B/860